A Nation In
Labour

HARRIET ANENA

PRAISE FOR A NATION IN LABOUR

"A Nation in Labour demonstrates the mystic ability of verse. This collection is a battle between our conscience and the social and political truths around us. Anena is a gift to the universe. I celebrate her tenacity and wit."
— **Beverley Nambozo Nsengiyunva| Poet, Author and Public Speaker.**

"Daring and innovative, Harriet Anena is well on the way to becoming one of the most important poets to come out of Africa in the last quarter of the century."
— **James Murua | Blogger & Journalist.**

"...a mature collection by a seasoned poet who displays the mastery of a wordsmith for whom words and lines of poetry are tools of the trade that don't intimidate her."
— **Prof. Laban Erapu | Author of Dominion.**

ISBN: 978-1511-6730-9-9

Layout & Design: Jackqueline Laker
Cover Illustration: Chrisogon Atukwasize

Set in Cambria & Garamond

Table of Contents

To Mama, for the inspiration
of your spoken poetry.

Foreword

This is not a conventional collection of poems by a young untried poet cautiously taking her first steps into the profession. It is a mature collection by a seasoned poet who displays the mastery of a wordsmith for whom words and lines of poetry are tools of the trade that don't intimidate her.

Poetry is an art that scares some people because they are not used to seeing beyond the words on a page. Its form and content raise a lot of questions that some readers don't feel confident enough to engage with. People looking for obvious answers should not read poems.

Poetry is not for the faint-hearted but for those who are willing to plunge in and become a part of it all. Those are the people for whom Harriet Anena writes with all her heart and soul!

It is not the pain and suffering which were the midwives to these poems that make them significant. What makes this an outstanding collection of poems is the valiant spirit that is the godfather of this prodigious talent that eloquently speaks for itself from the first page to the last.

I am proud to be a part of this work and humbled to have been asked to witness its birth.

Professor Laban Erapu
Bishop Stuart University Mbarara
18th January 2015

Skeletons of Laughter

We Planted Lies

We planted lies in our backyard
& they grew into mountains
that now tumble on our heads
like landslides of Bududa.

Walking on Nails

We're ashamed
of being afraid,
scared of tomorrow
even when today is still an infant.

We suit-up lies;
the truth scorches our tongues.

We curse the world
for sitting on our backs
& screwing our heads.

We blame the past
for bruising our present,
holding us at ransom
& jailing our future.

We gloat in mischief;
modesty demeans us,
withers our ego.

But, we lament
over our stunted progress;
strangle life
hammer nails into its head
as we strut,
onward.

Skeletons of Laughter

We search mass graves
in our hearts
for skeletons of laughter
that lay cold,
broken.

Salvation Rope

I pulled it tight
to the point of a snap;
my relief depended on it,
survival dangled from it;
this salvation rope,
hugging a stomach thirsty
for an occupant.

I picked red ants from the hill,
ignored their pinch
& filled my mouth.

In my mind, I was at table
with those who rule this land.

Food for the Hungry

On the pavement
with hands outstretched,
he waits.

The drizzle taps
his palms first.

He shivers. He waits.

The man in a pinstripe suit,
woman in heels,
don't look
his way.

Hunger stops by first,
tummy throbs. He hopes
for a slice of anything
edible.
Hands slouch,
head stoops.

A girl stops by,
something in hand.
He looks up,
smiles a thank you.

She watches
his jaws dance.
He watches
her leave.

Let's Leave

Take me
to a place green
& clean;
where smiles
rise from the bed
of bellies;
& laughter
holds no pity.

Let's flee
to breathe
air undefiled
& live life
unpolluted.

When I Became a Cow

I was reborn
a cow,
the day he gifted my people
a kraal
for my hand.

My daughter will be reborn
a fridge,
the day her man empties his bank account
in my palms.

I get slaps
& canes
for opening my mouth.
My daughter will get whips
of silence
from the man
she'll call *my man*.

The Last Cry

Life sat
on my palms
& looked me in the eye.

I looked back.

We smiled. Laughed.
Then it seeped
through my fingers.

A scream
escaped
my mouth
& I salvaged
the last drop.

Stuck

We obey
unsaid commands,
kill words
at birth,
hospitalise reality &
narrate erased histories.

We beseech buried idols
to salvage compromised futures
& wait for the sun to break
our silence.

January Blues

The stomach weeps
as it recalls memories
of satisfaction.

The pocket holds onto goodbye
jingles of coins spent
in moments
of exhilaration.

You want to think
outside the box
& return to normalcy.
You see no box.

You wait
& begin the countdown
away from January Blues.

Running

I need to flee
to a place distant
& mysterious;
where I'll see no faces
hear no voices
smell & taste nothing,
touch & be touched
by nobody.

I need to flee,
& retrace my steps
to myself.

Sea Jigger

I lust for the Sea,
strip for its breeze
to taste my skin.

I ache for the shore,
surrender to its pebbles
to lick my feet.

I drip. I drift.
Waves woo me.

The Sea moans
sounds of seduction &
at once, I'm Moses,
at the Red Sea,
fleeing Pharaoh;
a Sea Jigger,
HIV.

We Are On Heat

Hemline Cop

You stand at the street corner
eyes darting.

You swallow
hard;
tongue wet.

Your eyes strip me
& scream *Malaya!*

Your hemline court
finds me guilty
of indecency.

Undress her!

Your disciples descend
like bees awakened
from their hive.

The stench
of your jail cell
gags me.

I can't breathe,
but I dig
into the walls.

Lest We Forget To Fear

Fear not,
even the holy book says so.

So we fear not &
press the detonate button.

We fear not &
loot the communal pot.

Fear not,
even the holy book says so.

So we fear not.

Kiwani

It used to be raw,
unmasked.

Now I wrap it,
profess the diluted,
the *kiwani* love
that could even be hate.

Relics

My fingers hesitate
at the thought of typing
I Miss You.

Wanting you
scares me to perspiration,
but my tongue still recalls
the taste of peak moments.

I won't inscribe
goodbye on the grave
bearing memories of you;
my hands won't rise
to hit the last nail.

I spectate
as you roam my mind,
begging for relics
of what almost was.

Disobedient

I discarded the rules,
made the declaration
placed my claim
on a man.

On this Black Dress

She's wearing black today;
not for the darkness of the moment
but for the thickness of memory.

On this black dress are footprints
of eyes that trailed her face,
lingered
on her neck & proceeded...
downwards;
eyes that shone
like glow-worms
on a moody night.

On this black dress is a memory
of light that lit her face
when he held her shoulders,
drew her close &
she'd melted in his arms.

On this black dress
is a memory
that now rolls like
a ball of fire
on her wet face.

Waltzing Tongues

Your tongue
waltzes on mine until
I surrender the body
you've drawn maps on;
complete with rivers
valleys
hills.

Now your eyes
are red suns
raying my chest.

I take a deep breath
that may well be the last.

Breathless Mount

Shrubs stroke my feet,
the slope sucks my breath.

The peak beckons,
the end entices.

I hold out my hand
to grab it – life after here.

NO, it says.
I'm not yours to touch (yet).

I Won't

I won't bow
for your decree
to keep my head
down.

Absent

We kiss imaginary lips,
hug absent bodies,
bow to distance,
surrender to absence.

We smile smiles unrequited,
dream
yearn
alone
silently.

V-Day

I

Marry me.
The words nearly miss your ears,
land in your heart with a thud.

You freeze.
Eyes let go of tears
quickly summoned.
Yes becomes too heavy
a word to utter.
Chest thuds with the energy
of a *bwola* dancer,
stomach dances to a parade
of butterflies.

II

It's over.
The words strike within,
you shrink,
don't ask why.
Mouth says *it's fine*;
eyes know it isn't.

III
You wait
for no one in particular,
hope they'll drop by,
say the right things &
ask the right questions.

Nobody passes by,
so you buy a rose
go on a date
drink four shots
of U.G.

You dance,
kiss your lips,
savour your company.

It's just another day
& you are still you.

We Are On Heat

We cry & kiss
at the same time as
our eyes gleam
with longing
& hesitation.

We run to heaven & hell
at the same time as
our hearts pulse
with joy
& pain.

We are on heat
like cows on a vibrator;
then we stop &
breathe & conquer
militant things within.

Say It

Today, I'll let your breath
kiss my neck,
arms encircle my waist
words stroke my ears.

I'll let your fingers wander
in my hair,
eyes take in
my body
as I wait
for you
to say it.

And I Die, Many Times Over

My knees quiver
like a drenched chick;
insides rumble
like mild thunder.

My heart sings
songs whose lyrics I barely know;
lips tremble
at the thought of yours.

I hear your voice
in my sleep. You seduce me
without trying &
I die,
many times over.

Mukeka

You knitted torn pieces
of my heart like mukeka.

Now we sit on the Kituba trunk
every evening;
you familiar-ing your ears
with a new rhythm
in my chest &
I, watching the sun
fall asleep
in your eyes.

Notes

I'm seated by the shore,
watching the sea
wash away notes
of touches,
warm wet kisses
& thrust of hips.

I'm standing by the shore,
screaming as the sea tears up
jotted names of children
yet to be conceived.

I'm running by the shore,
crying as the sea swallows up
shredded notes of bonds built
& words that once meant
Mapenzi wangu.
Lapalcwinya
My love!

We'll Plant Bullets

Un-weanable

He clings onto breasts
of the Republic,
squeezing,
biting them with 70-year-old teeth,
blind to the queue
of infants behind him.

Heroes

Guns fed on sons
we sent to catch the enemy
in Somalia.

Now we wait
for flag-wrapped caskets,
neat parade
21-gun salute.

We mourn,
& pray for cash rescue
from the chief mourner.

Tomorrow, he'll birth new wars
& wait for heroes
of our wombs
to fall.

Sharing my Man with a Country

I can't wait for you to leave
so that I can tell our daughter
that loving you,
was like trying to scoop the wind
with a basket.

I'll tell her I loved you
with my mouth shut;
I wasn't sure you wanted to hear me
speak, or coil in a corner
& smile for the dignitaries
from China.

I'll tell her I wrote
countless letters,
but I wasn't sure you'd read them
& call me sweet
like you sometimes did,
or smack my face
& call me petty
like you often do.

I can't wait for you to leave
so that I can tell our daughter,
never to have an affair
with a man,
whose first wife is a country.

The Political Returnee

He looked master in the eye
& saw a vision long blurred.

The convoy had veered off the road.

He fled the camp,
looked back & saw
a house long de-roofed.

There was no Movement.

The 10 Sacred Creed
lay beneath war boots.

He tore the menu-fasto
of deception,
wore black every Monday,
rallied the poor
to shame looters
of the Treasury.

But he's back in the brotherhood,
gifting his conscience
to the predator,
relearning songs they sang
in Luwero as they shot
their way to the top.

A Nation in Labour

The Republic is in labour,
screaming,
pacing the political ward,
cursing the colonial midwife
for telling her to push.

Her head is spinning,
vision blurred,
mind inside out.

She drinks counterfeit morality
& blubbers a prayer of hope
for the stillborn baby.

The Republic is a headless chicken
with a body that can only flip
& flap in labour.

She curses the future
for coming too soon,
clings onto a grandfather clock
that's out of tune,
hoping it'll correct a future
that's gone askew.

New-born Dreams

She comes bearing a basket
of dreams you've not dreamt,
takes a seat on your tok-tok,
washes scabs of failure
off your hands & serves hope
at supper.

You smile. Breathe
dream, but up north,
love is on a death bed,
hatred is breast-fed,
hypocrisy is obese &
the gun stutters like the people
doomed to dance its tune.

Tomorrow, the sun will sprinkle rays;
dark skies will clear up,
angry winds will calm down.

New-born dreams
will appear in the horizon.

War Worms

We found South Sudan choking
on blood
from its birth.

We sang:
kill tribal worms
heal ancient wounds
sieve spiteful words
denounce neck-twisting
stop war-cheering.

We found South Sudan limping
from the ache
of war wounds.

We sang:
kill fires of fury
shame aides of hate
bury Satans of destruction.

Rebuild home
with hands that pulled triggers;
grow food
in fields that shielded enemies;
manure the land
that only knew blood.

This State need not die
at birth,
no one should dread home.

We found South Sudan munching
on a poisonous war.

We said:
stop
& limp
to the finish line.

Did you (also) speak?

Twin Pregnancy

He's pregnant again
with a set of twin corruption.

He sunbathes atop the hill,
as the weight of plundered goods
keeps him still.

The wananchi — pregnant too—
looks up from the valley,
gnashes teeth in labour pains
that's been on for 53 years.

Don't waste your time
with inducement or C-section;
there's nothing inside.

Take photos of their legs —
the size of infant tree stems;
zoom onto their belly —
distended with emptiness;
focus on their eyes —
bright with deficiency
of hope.

Political Poop

We scramble for sachets
of salt & pennies
from county gods
as we tighten grips
on each other's necks.

We kneel to hear
blessed words
from the man in-charge
& replace our history
with made-up truths.

Political poop splashes
on our faces
as we clamor for crumbs
from overloaded tables.

A whip lands,
bullets fly,
teargas fumes the air
as we dive
head first,
into our life's puke.

Oath of Patriotism

He trembles like a leaf
in June when he sees her;
palms sweaty with desire
like the face of a courtship dancer.

He wants to *eat* her
but doesn't know where to start
so he whips her,
locks her up in a *safe* house.

He gets to his knees,
crawls like a child looking
for lost candy,
& sheds tears made in Beijing.

He moans;
this shouldn't have happened,
I just needed your word,
your oath of patriotism.

We'll Plant Bullets

He said the teeth of our hoes
can't bite the soil anymore.
He supplied AK47 instead,
to clear hostile vegetation.

He said the farmer is clueless
about his trade. He deployed
the men in uniform instead,
to drain life out of wetlands
& make way for shopping malls.

He said our seeds are unresponsive
to modern manure.
He planted bullets instead,
promised a mega harvest
of patriotism
to cure our hunger.

Tears and Laughter

Flames waved at us yesterday;
made ash out of everything
we held dear
& dared our voices to rise
above the carnage.

We dreamt of sacks of cash
tucked under *their* pillows;
remnants of the national cake
sprinkled under their tables.

The sun rose
& we held onto hollow hope
of rebuilding our nation
on a foundation of ashes.

I Bow for My Boobs

We Arise

we came. we went.
we have come again.

we stand. we stroll.
we search, this field
where trees sheltered us.

we talk. we argue.
we laugh in this swamp
where mosquitoes
gave us company.

we sit. we watch.
we ponder about this home
where history changed hue
from light to dark.

we share. we memorize.
we recall weeks of running,
months of falling,
years of rising up.

We learn,
from decades of fleeing our homes,
dodging pricks from *okutu lango*
avoiding tumbles on *dul yen*
tearing through thickets of *agaba*
freeing our feet from marshy *kulu*.

Today we rise
& stand tall.

I Bow for my Boobs

Ojok is back
stinking of arege
another bottle in hand
like his life depends on it.

The colour of his eyes compete
with the redness of a ripe
kamlara.

Trousers hang low,
wet at the groin
down to his knees,
belt unbuckled.

He growls like a dog
protecting its bone.

I tiptoe into the house
stand before the mirror
naked.
I pray to my breasts,
touching them I whisper:
turn into stones
pelt my husband
send him to the grave
be my weapon of destruction.

A Rotten Forgiveness

The rim of a gun is on my forehead.
I feel a bullet run through
even before the trigger
is pulled.

I don't flinch.

We wronged you, killed your mother,
your father, your sister, your brother,
they say.

They don't say that I was killed too;
don't know I'm a cracked shell.

They can't fathom why
my body doesn't quiver
at the sight of guns anymore.

They don't know that death plays
in my head daily.

We can't bring back lives lost. Spit out
the anger, swallow the hurt, they say.

I dig up memories & names
from beneath my tongue
& hurl
damnation
unto their faces.

A Nod to Death*

She chews with such care
you'd think the food
feels pain too.

Sores coat her mouth
like cow dung on a mud wall.

This pain comes with a nod,
eats flesh from bone,
loosens the tap of saliva.

She chews with care
swallows slowly,
nodding to a grave
already dug.

*In memory of children who died of the
Nodding Syndrome in Northern Uganda.*

Silent Ears

I see them,
hear them laugh:
the children
Amaa & Abaa,
even the unborn.

I didn't heed them then,
didn't feel their pain;
what made me human was blown up
by explosives planted by Kony
& his men.

I seek to undo the slaughter,
re-sculpture the dead.

I long for a conversation,
but my plea, like theirs then,
falls on silent ears.

Unafraid

A marabou stork tiptoes on bones
of shoe-less corpses in Pagak.

Red Cross hands out blue cups
of yellow porridge
in Unyama Camp.

Women climb roof tops
with thatch on their backs
in Laliya Village.

Men gulp litres of *kill-me-quick*
in Adak Trading Center.

In Gulu Town, a mob forms
a ring around a man in black.
He won't drop the snatched bag.

A tyre falls on his head
body soaks in petrol.
 A match is lit.

He sings
his mother's name
as flames engulf him.

Tomorrow, *they* will say
there was no time
to dig a grave.

Scratching Destiny

The sun rises
& sheds its radiance
onto the earth.

The wind blows
across hills & valleys,
over rocks & mountains;
bringing hope & joy
to everyone on earth.

But not so for the Acoli child
born in the bush
living in IDP camps
year in, year out,
20 and over.

Surrounded by terror
in a land of misfortune.

Weeping & wailing
mourning & groaning
are your life's companion.

AIDS robbed you
of parental love & care.
You face brutality
abduction
& is sexually molested
by your *protectors.*

The investor salivates
for your land
but still, you scratch
your destiny
from hands
of a curtailing fate.

Footprints of Memory

I sit on the lap
of a dung-smeared floor
& inhale the scent
of aging smoke.

I rest my head on chest
of a mud wall,
listen to sounds lodged
between bricks;
bricks fractured
by desertion &
footprints of memory.

I stand at the door
of a grass-thatched hut
that was my maternity ward;
a hut whose floor drank
blood of my motherhood
as I brought forth life;
life that now roams the world
like disciples
of al-Qaeda:
picking &
plundering.

I Envy the Dead

I stand on the edge
of Got Moro, listening to voices
chorusing
jump! don't!

My mind travels a year back,
when Otti gave me a panga
& bellowed, *take her home!*

He should have told me to take *them home.*
Mother was carrying another life.

What are you waiting for?

I wanted to give him the weapon
but he would've taken me *home* first.
I didn't want to go *home* yet,
I needed to remind him
someday about this day.

I closed my eyes
& struck.

Now I stand
on the edge of Got Moro,
envying the dead
whose graveyards are unmarked.

Forgiveness

Mama's tongue was chopped
& dropped in the pot
that cooked our *dek ngor*.

Akec was snatched
from Mama's nipples &
thrust against a tree.

Papa's lips were sealed
with padlocks
meant for *their* jail cells.

God & his son sat sky-high
watching
as our homes were torched
by men-turned-beasts.

You tell me to forgive
& all I see are heaps of sand
sitting mockingly
on remnants of my kin.

I Died Alive

A voice resounded
within, inner eye watched
the outside, agile dreams
took me
miles away.

I died.
I died alive.

Anew

I want to uproot a seedling
that sits within;
replant myself
on fallowed land;
erase my beginning,
unwrite my history.

I want to unknow,
enthrone my soul
on a beginning
devoid of sweetened lies
& concealed hate.

I yearn to lay a foundation
of newness:
      a new now
      a new tomorrow
      a new after tomorrow.

Friends

We laugh from places apart;
the loud, rare laughter
that carries the echo
of a patented bond.

We smile at silly little things
that mean so much:
the rants & real talks
& seriousness & brilliance,
the counsel that comes out light
& yet so heavy.

We yearn for what is better felt;
dream of forest walks, tree climbs
& gambles with food recipes.

We relish each minute,
even from places apart;
you, there
me, here.

Acknowledgements

Great appreciation to those who believed in my poetry from the first encounter: Bob G. Kisiki, Caroline Ayugi, Richard Ugbede Ali and Prof. Laban Erapu.

Gratitude to Hellen Aluku — you tireless morale-booster of my writing, and Nyana Kakoma for your support, always!

Thank you Dad, reader of my words, long before I could write; these letters are yours too.

Uganda, the ingredients for this collection came from you. Apwoyo!

About the Author

Harriet Anena from Gulu, i Uganda.

Her fiction stories and poems have been published or are forthcoming in the Caine Prize anthology, Jalada Africa, New Daughters of Africa anthology, Short Story Day Africa's *ID* and *Hotel* anthologies, FEMRITE and Babishai Niwe Poetry anthologies, Sooo Many Stories, Adda, Storymoja Publishers among others.

Her works have been nominated for the Commonwealth Short Story Prize, Short Story Day Africa Prize and the Ghana Poetry Prize (2013).

Made in the USA
Lexington, KY
10 December 2019